HANDSHADOWS FOR KIDS

JB Books Ltd 2017

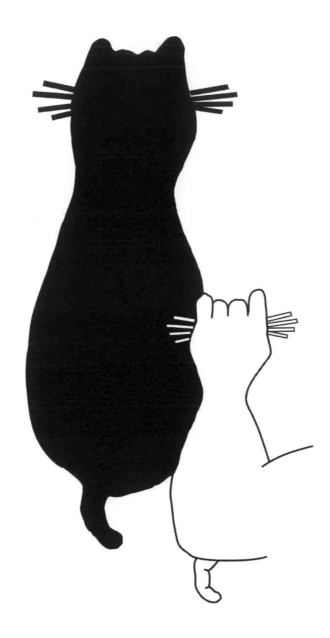

Cat

Spider

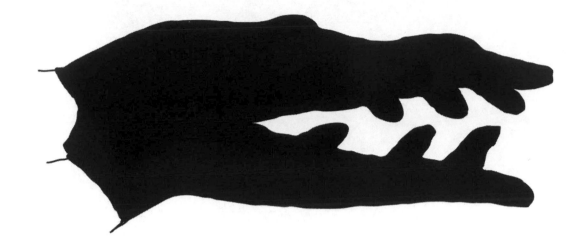

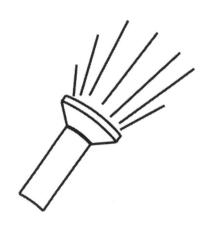

Crocodile

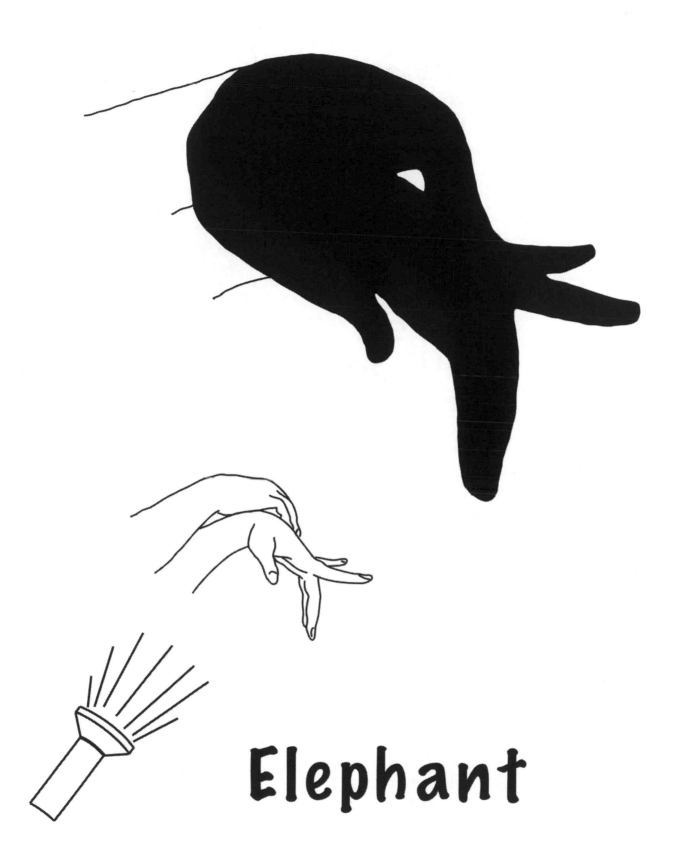

Elephant

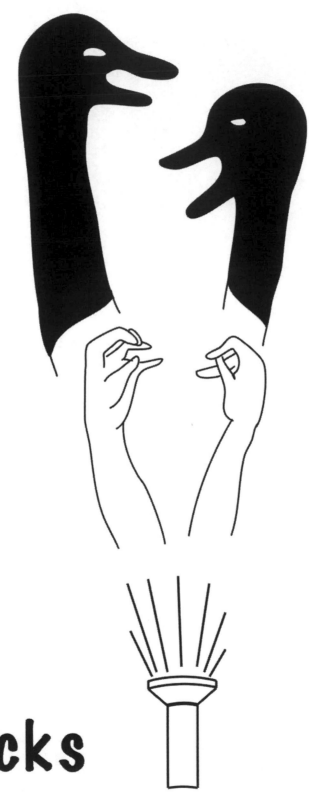

Ducks

Crow

Cowboy

Parrot

Caribou

Puppy

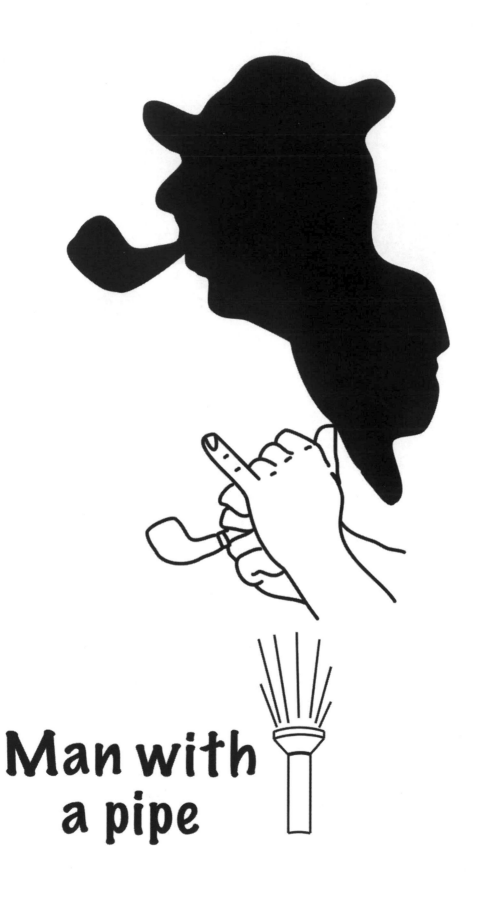

Man with
a pipe

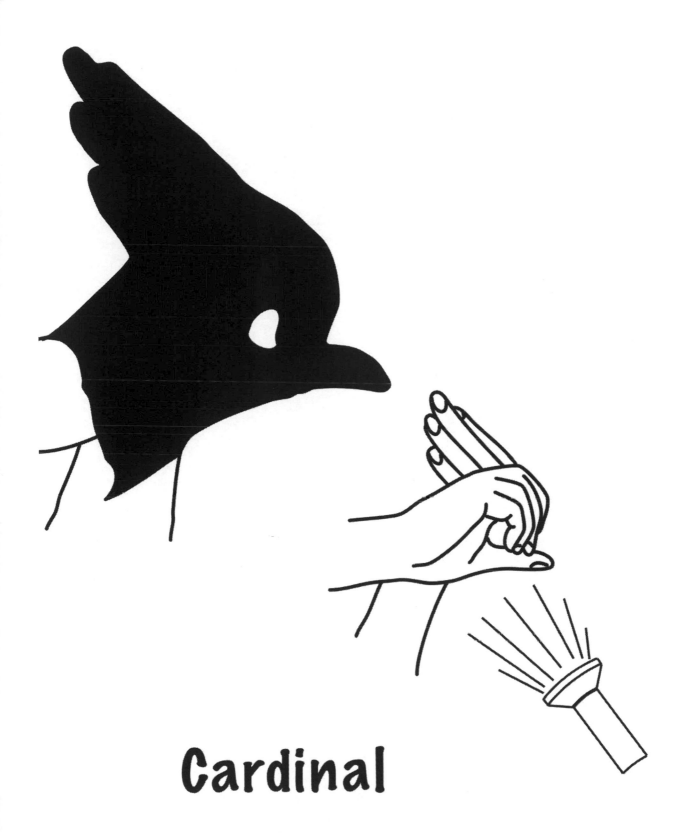

Cardinal

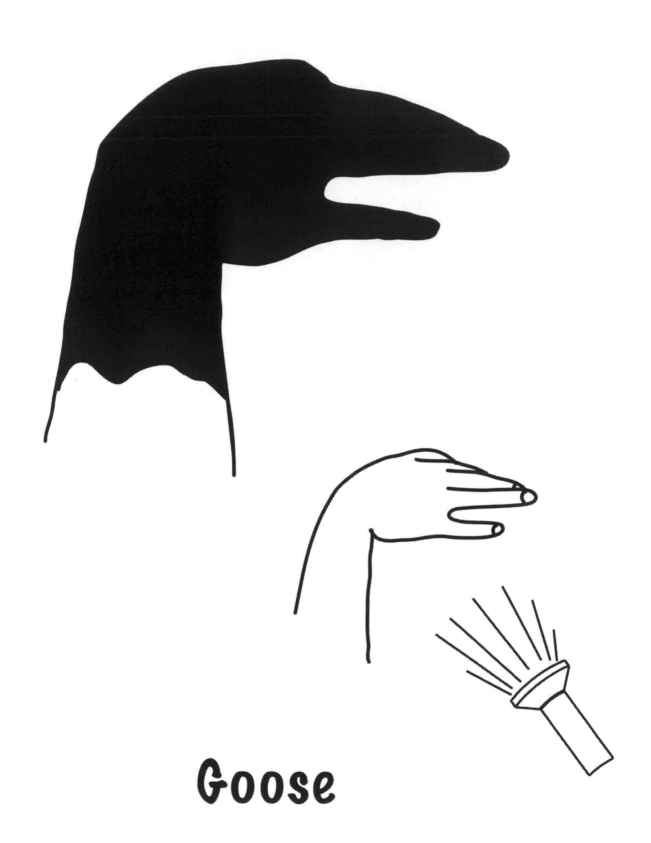

Goose

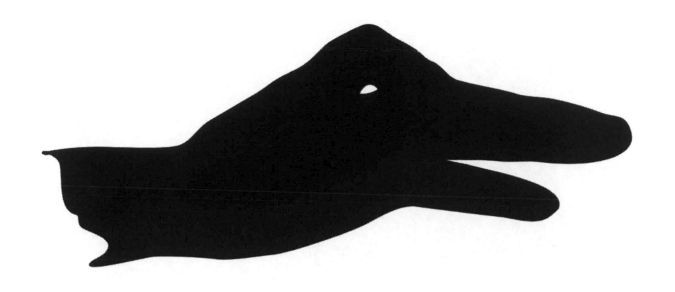

Goose 2

Goat

Donkey

Chamois

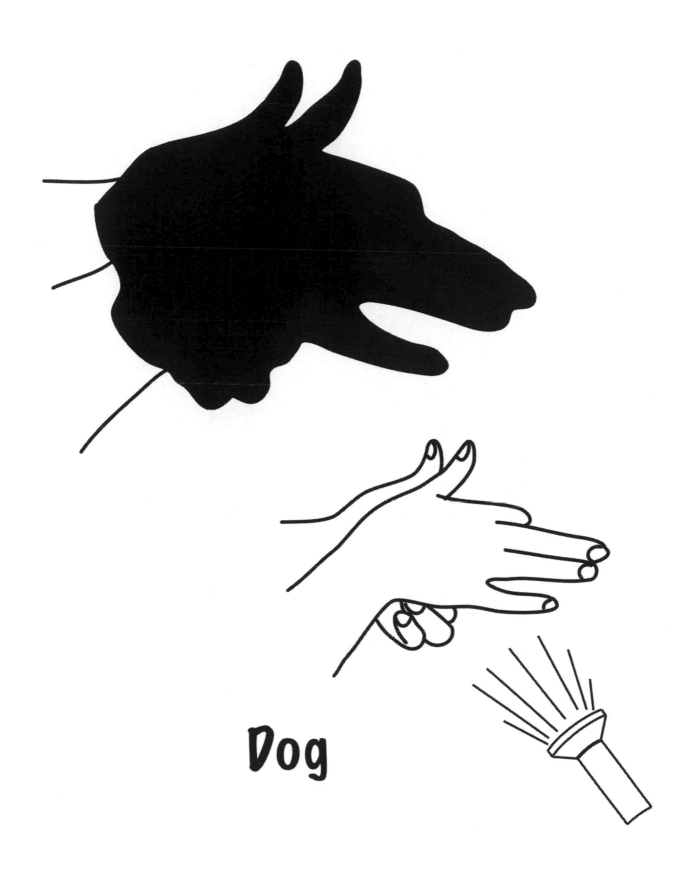

Dog

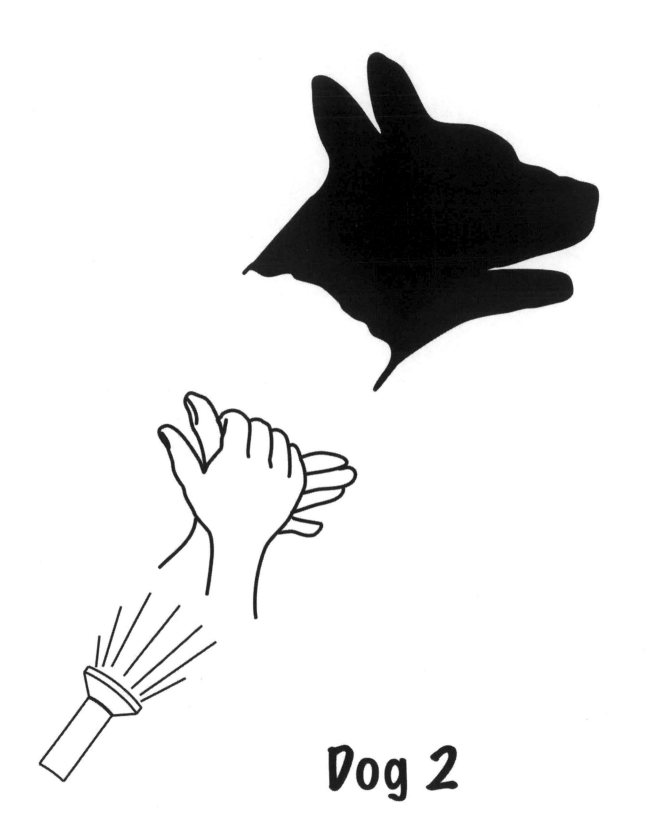

Dog 2

Turtle

Ostrich

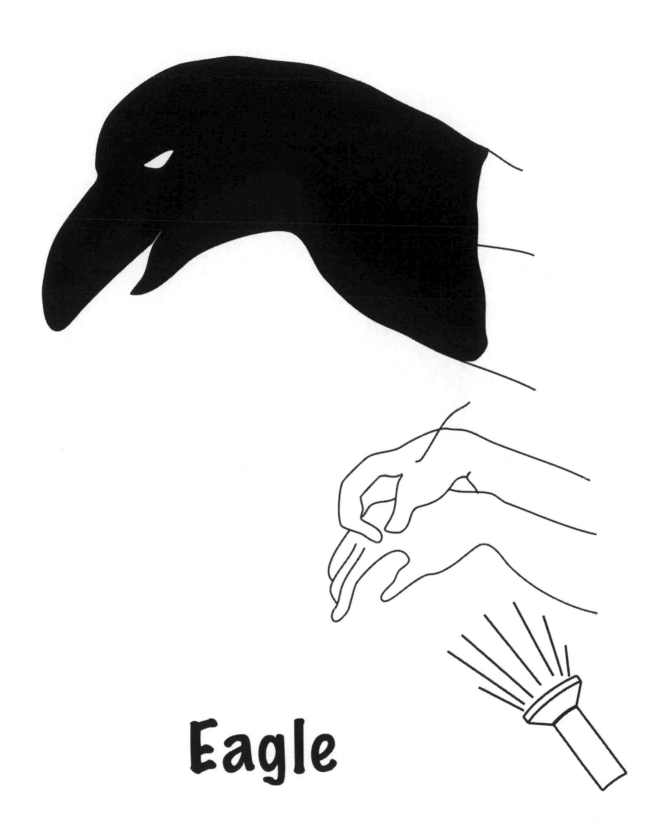

Eagle

Kangaroo

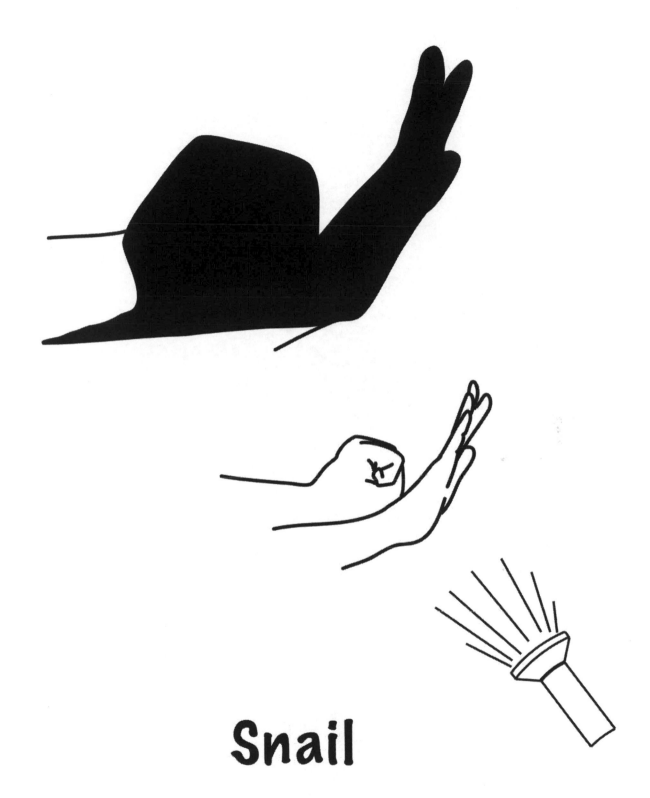

Snail

Reindeer

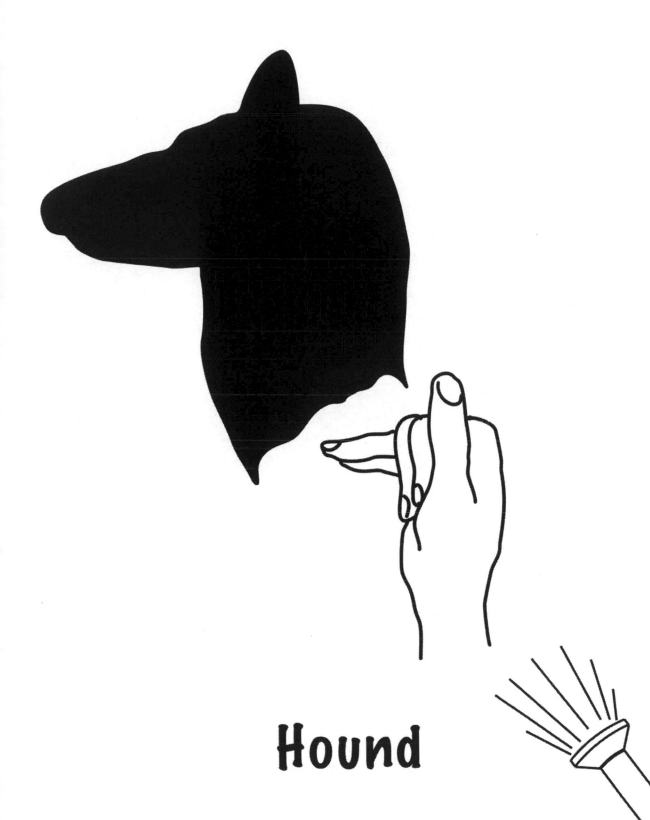

Hound

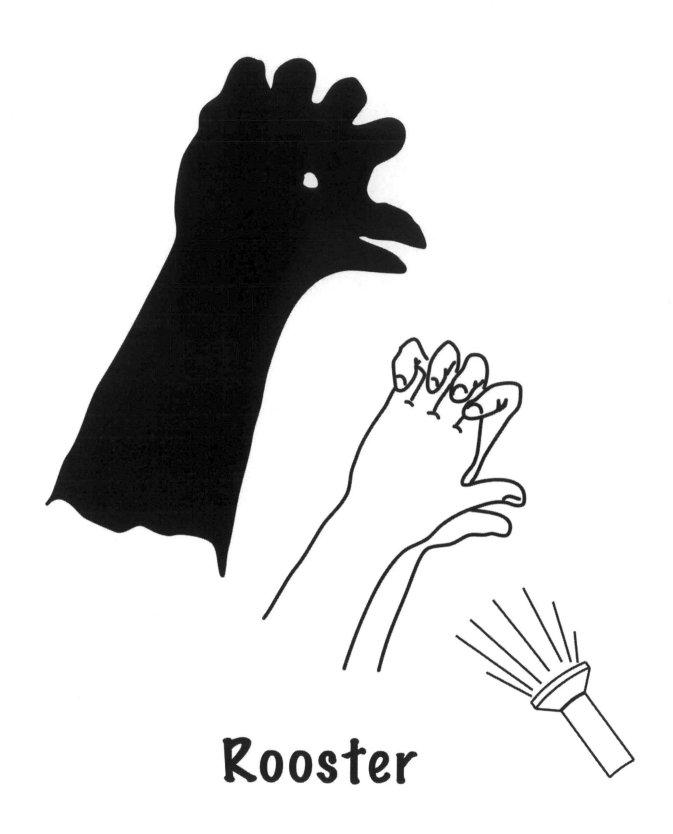

Rooster

Rabbit

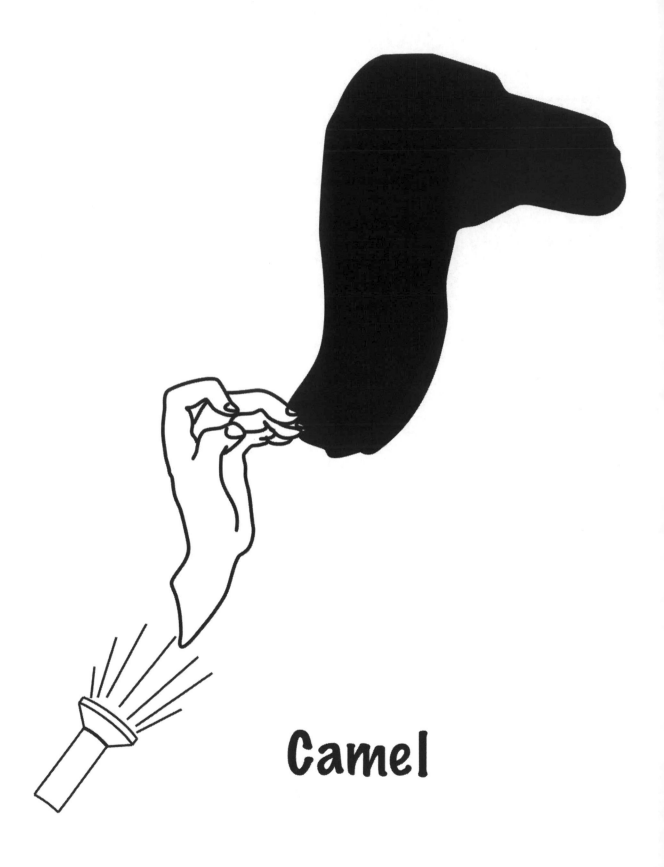

Camel

Camel 2

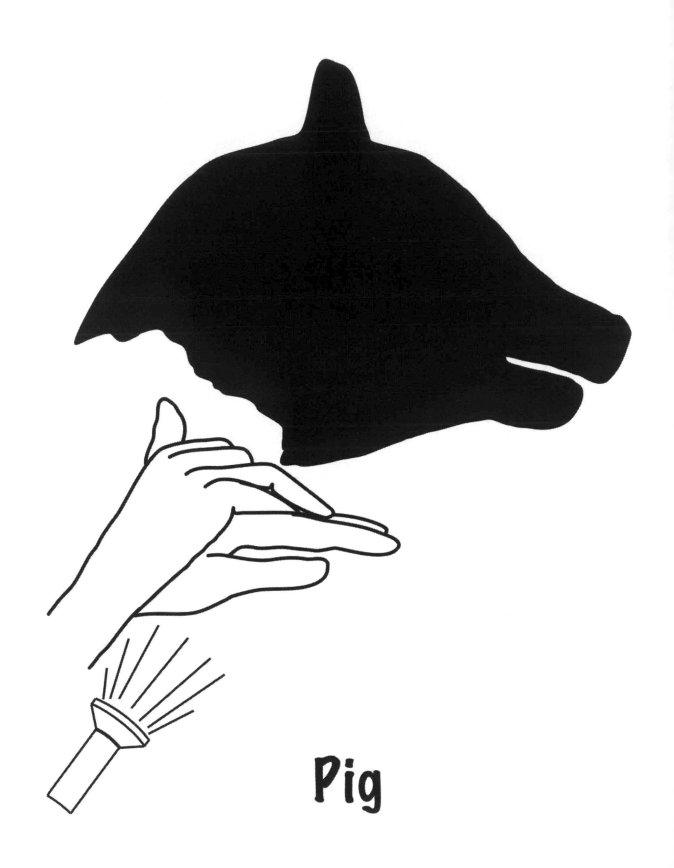

Pig

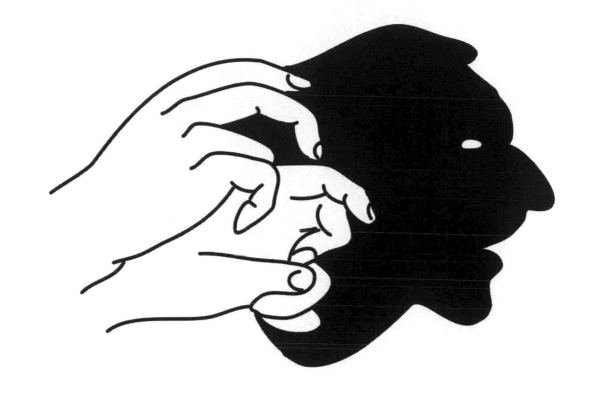

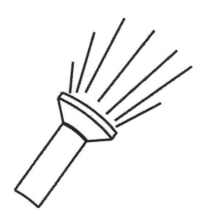

Man's Face

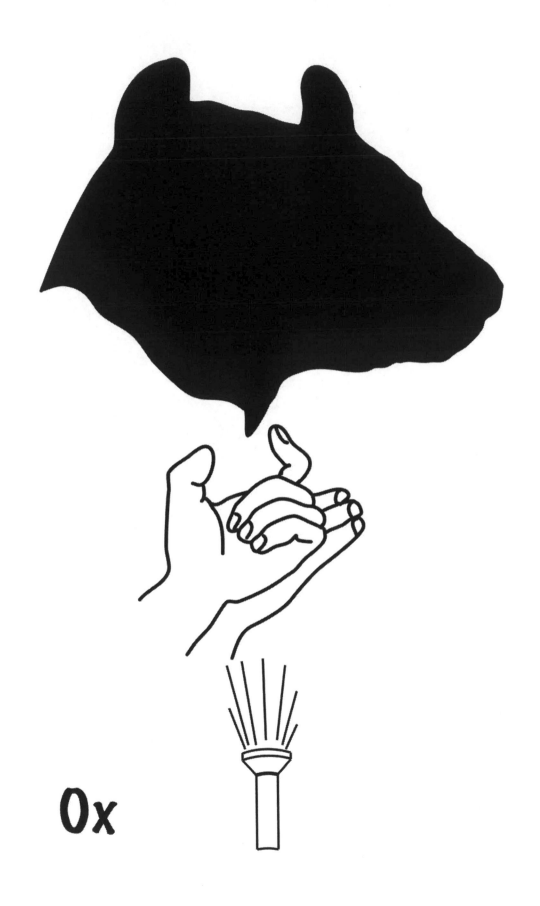

0x

Bear

American Indian

Bird

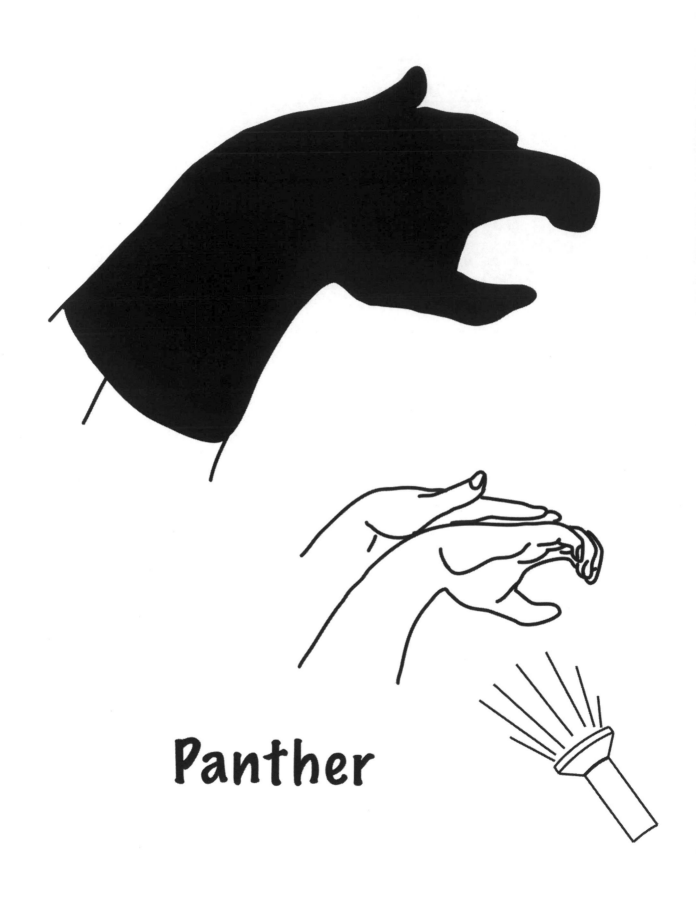

Panther

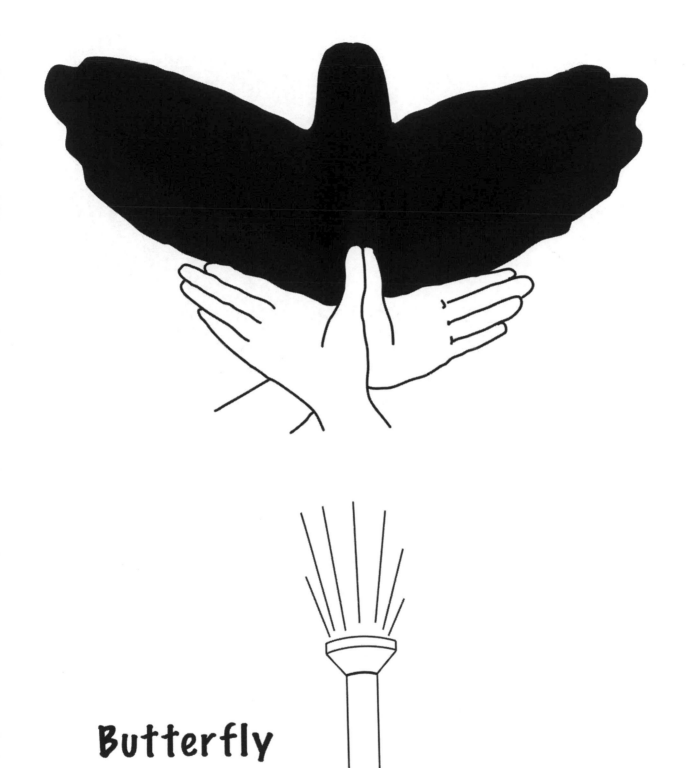

Butterfly

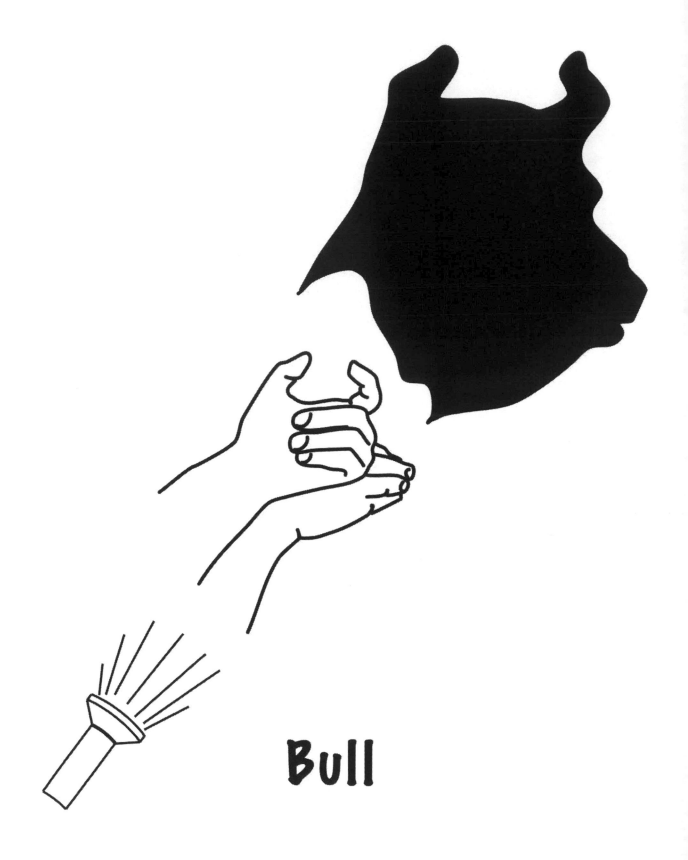

Bull

Turkey

Fox

Growling Wolf

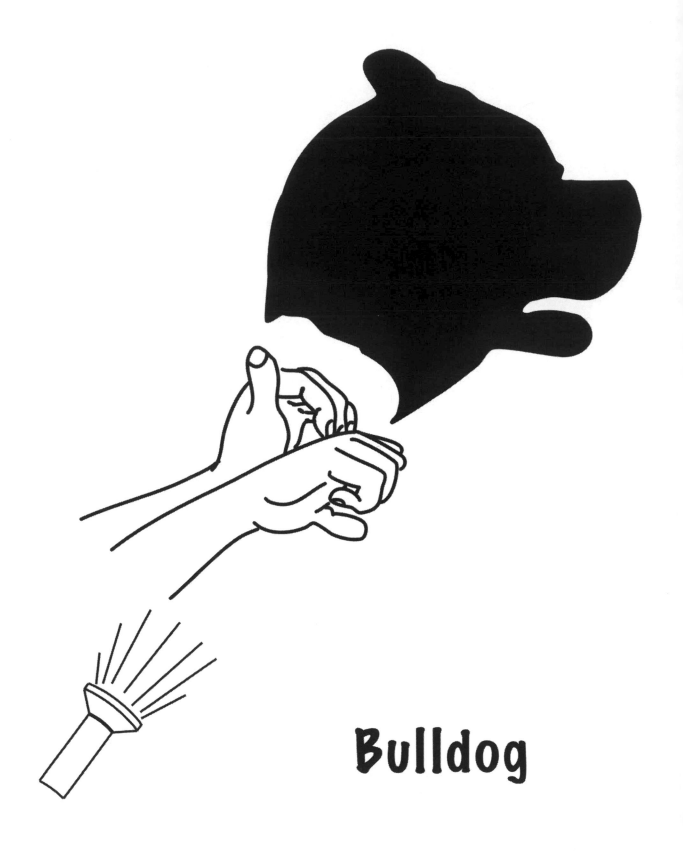

Bulldog

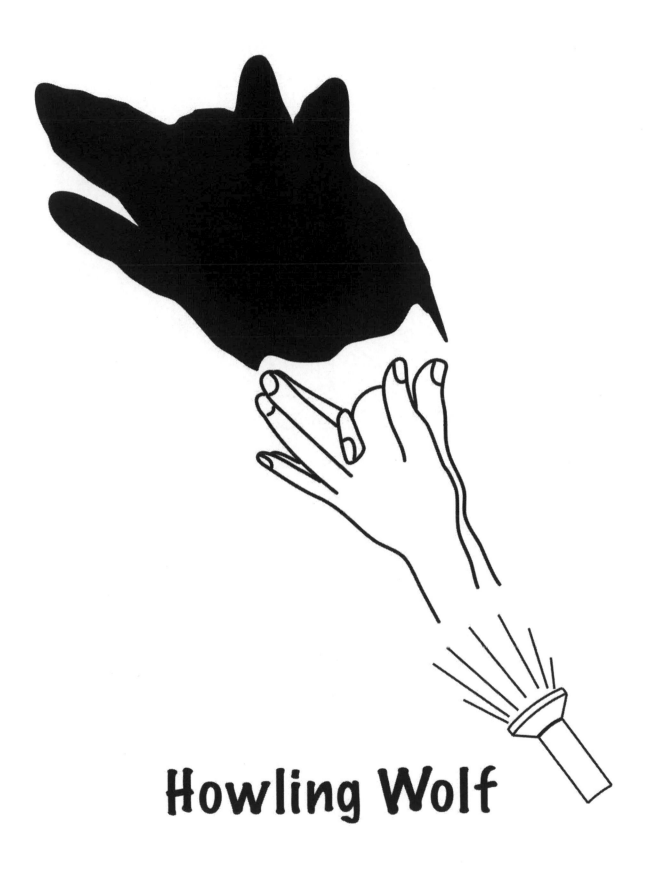

Howling Wolf